Experiments with
PLANTS AND
OTHER LIVING THINGS

TREVOR COOK

PowerKiDS
press.

New York

Published in 2009 by The Rosen Publishing Group, Inc.
29 East 21st Street, New York, NY 10010

Editor: Alex Woolf
Designers: Sally Henry and Trevor Cook
Consultant: Keith Clayson
U.S. Editor: Kara Murray

Picture Credits: Sally Henry and Trevor Cook

Every attempt has been made to clear copyright. Should there be any
inadvertent omission, please apply to the publisher for rectification.

Library of Congress Cataloging-in-Publication Data

Cook, Trevor, 1948–
   Experiments with plants and other living things / Trevor Cook.
      p. cm. — (Science lab)
   Includes index.
   ISBN 978-1-4358-2806-3 (library binding) — ISBN 978-1-4358-3219-0 (pbk.)
ISBN 978-1-4042-8024-3 (6-pack)
   1. Plants—Experiments—Juvenile literature. 2. Biology—Experiments—
Juvenile literature. I. Title.
   QK52.6.C66 2009
   570.78—dc22
                                           2008036895
5958
Printed in the United States

Contents

Introduction

Living things include the plants, animals, *fungi* and algae that we can see, as well as the tiny organisms such as *bacteria* and protozoa that can be seen only with a microscope. These organisms live in every type of place on Earth – on land and in lakes, rivers and seas. Some organisms, such as some worms, bacteria and protozoa, live in both water and soil.

Arctic lupin

The record for the world's oldest germinated seed is an Arctic lupin (*Lupinus arcticus*). Found in a lemming *burrow* in frozen Arctic tundra, the seed actually germinated and flowered after about 10,000 years!

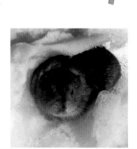

Lemming in burrow

Rafflesia flower

Scientists think that there are over a million kinds of fungi in the world, but only about 10 percent have been properly described.

Fungus

The rain forests of Borneo are home to the world's biggest flower, called the rafflesia. It's a parasitic plant with no stem or leaves but with roots buried in its host vine. It needs flies to spread its pollen to other flowers, so it draws them to it by producing the smell of rotting meat!

Man belongs to a group of animals called mammals. The smallest member of the group is possibly the Kitti's hog-nosed bat, from Thailand, which weighs about 1 ounce (2 g) and is around .5 inch (12 mm) long. The largest is likely the blue whale, weighing up to 370,000 pounds (170,000 kg) and measuring around 108 feet (33 m) long!

Blue whale

Kitti's hog-nosed bat

Algae

Algae used to be considered a kind of simple plant but are now seen as a necessary and complex part of the life in our world. Algae have *chlorophyll*, like plants, and manufacture their own food from *nutrients* and sunlight.

Another record for survival is the Asian water lotus (*Nelumbo nucifera*). A seed from China was grown after 1,200 years.

Asian water lotus

Bacteria are a very simple form of life, but they can really *thrive* in the surroundings to which they are adapted.

Bacteria grown in the laboratory

Friends can help…
Do the experiments with your friends!

Jargon Buster
A **mammal** is an animal that has a backbone, hair or fur and gives birth to live young, which it feeds with milk.

Some technical or unusual words, shown in *italic* type, are explained in the glossary on page 31.

Materials and Tools

You should easily find many things that you need for our experiments around your home.

20 minutes This tells you about how long a project should take.

 This symbol means you might need adult help.

Tape We use tape to hold things in position. Masking tape or clear packing tape will do.

Waterproof tape When we need  to make stronger connections, it's best to use thicker, waterproof tape sometimes called duct tape.

Glue stick is mostly used for sticking paper to paper. Rubber cement is a rubbery glue that sticks most things to most other things!

Scissors Ask an adult for an old pair of scissors that you can keep for all your experiments. They will be very useful. Keep them away from young children.

Plastic dropper It is available from arts and crafts shops and is ideal for controlling drops of liquid.

String Ordinary household string will be fine for most of our needs.

Funnel It is very useful for filtering liquids when used with coffee filters or paper towels and is also handy when filling bottles. We also use funnels with sound! See page 26.

Tubes Collect cardboard tubes from paper towels or other paper rolls to use in experiments.

Food coloring Small bottles of food coloring, or dye, are available from supermarkets for coloring cakes and other sweets. It's very strong. You will need only a few drops. Avoid getting dye on your clothes!

Plastic bottles Ask an adult for empty plastic bottles. The ones used for water and soda are best.

Popsicle sticks These are ideal for stirring mixtures or lighting tea lights. Collect them next time you eat popsicles!

Jars Try to save as many different clean, empty jars at home as you can. We are going to need quite a few for the experiments. Afterward you can recycle them.

Kitchen supplies Be careful when using food or anything from unmarked bottles. Check with an adult and get permission first.

Notebook Keep a special notebook to *record* the results of your experiments.

Shoe box Every time someone buys new shoes, there might be a box available. Save them for your experiments. Tissue boxes can also be handy. See page 16.

Watering can See if you can find a small watering can. It would be ideal for keeping your seeds and seedlings watered.

Paper towels Paper towels on a roll are very useful for cleaning up and required for quite a few of our experiments.

What Do Seeds Need to Grow?

Many plants spread themselves by *scattering* seeds. A seed holds a new plant and enough food for it to start growing inside it.

preparation 20 minutes

You will need:

- paper towel
- thick cardboard
- 4 clean, shallow trays
- quick-germinating seeds, such as cress
- water

The plan

We are going to find out what a seed needs to germinate. Does it need water, light and warmth? Collect some trays for this project.

What to do:

1 Put three or four thicknesses of paper towel in the bottom of each tray. Scatter the same number of seeds in each tray. Label them A, B, C, D. Wet the paper towels in trays A, B and C.

A	B	C	D
has everything	no warmth no light	no light	no water

2 Put trays A and D near a window in a warm room.

3 Cover tray C with thick cardboard to keep the light out and put it with A and D.

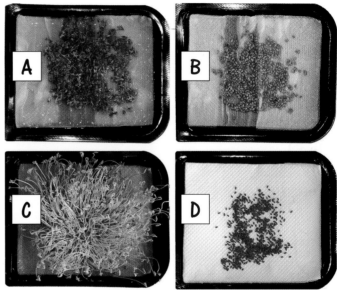

4 Put tray B in the fridge, to give no warmth.

5 Check the trays daily. After five days the seeds should look quite different.

What's going on?

Seeds won't germinate without water, but they don't need light. Without warmth, they grow more slowly or don't germinate at all.

What else can you do?

Keep the germinated seedlings in the same conditions and see if their needs are the same.

Plants and Gravity

Have you ever wondered why when you plant seeds, the roots always go down into the soil and the leaves up into the air?

preparation 25 minutes

You will need:

- 4 jars, broad-bean seeds
- some paper towels or blotting paper
- scissors, water

The plan

We're going to germinate some seeds in different positions to see which way the roots go.

start with four bean seeds from the packet

What to do:

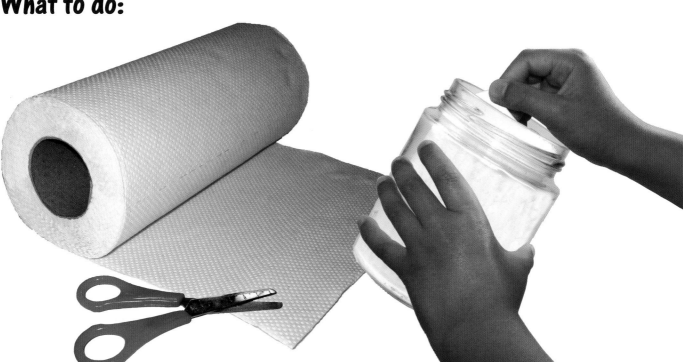

1 Cut a piece of paper towel or blotting paper to fit around the sides of the jar. It should be tight enough that it fits securely against the sides.

Jargon Buster
Germinate means begin to grow and put out shoots.

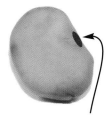

the black scar
where the bean
was connected
to its pod

2 Find the black scar on each seed. Put one seed in each jar, between the glass and the blotting paper.

Make each bean lie in a different direction. The first should lie with the scar up, the second with it down, the third with it to the left, the fourth to the right.

3 Put about 1 inch (25 mm) of water in each jar. It should soak into the paper to reach the seeds. Keep the water at this level.

What's going on?

The roots and the shoots always grow from the same point on the seed, but they react to *gravity*. Roots grow with gravity; shoots grow against gravity.

What else can you do?

After they have germinated, turn the seeds so that the roots are pointing upward and see what happens.

Transpiration

Plants get their water from the soil, but where does it go from there?

You will need:

- freshly cut white flowers, carnations are ideal
- glass of water, plastic dropper
- food coloring, scissors
- *magnifying glass*

The plan

We are going to see where water goes in plants by using dye to follow its path.

What to do:

1 Drop some food coloring into a glass of water.

2 Trim the flower stem before putting the flower into the water. Watch as the flower changes color.

3 You should get results that look like this!

giant redwood trees

What's going on?

Plant stems are made up of long, hollow cells like a series of straws.

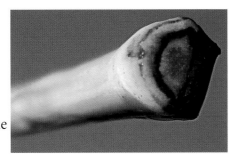

As water *evaporates* from the leaves, water is drawn up into the plant from the soil. This occurs in all plants. Giant redwood trees grow to over 300 feet (100 m) and draw water up their trunks in this way.

Jargon Buster

Transpiration means evaporation from leaves drawing water into a plant.

What else can you do?

Try dyeing colored flowers and see what new colors you get, test a red flower and green dye. Use a magnifying glass to examine flower stems to check them out close up!

What Do Plants Prefer?

Have you ever wondered if plants have a *preference* for what they grow in? By testing with *seedlings*, we try to find out when they grow best.

45 minutes

You will need:

- 4 same-size seedlings
- 4 similar containers
- *compost*, sand, gravel, soil
- water, labels, pen, notebook

The plan

We are going to see how seedlings *develop* when planted in different types of growing material.

What to do:

1 Put compost, sand, gravel and garden soil into similar-sized containers. We have used clean jars.

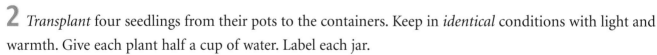

2 *Transplant* four seedlings from their pots to the containers. Keep in *identical* conditions with light and warmth. Give each plant half a cup of water. Label each jar.

compost

sand

gravel

soil

3 After a week you should be able to see clearly which plants are thriving or failing. Do you know why?

4 Remove the best-growing plant from the jar to check the root structure. Notice that both the leaves and the roots are developing well. This plant likes the conditions you have provided.

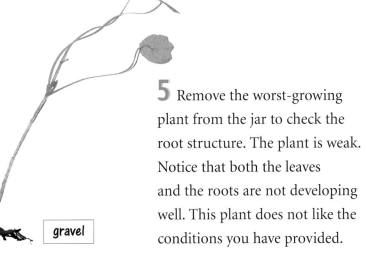

5 Remove the worst-growing plant from the jar to check the root structure. The plant is weak. Notice that both the leaves and the roots are not developing well. This plant does not like the conditions you have provided.

What's going on?

Results should prove that plants prefer a mixed material to grow in, such as garden soil or compost. Some compost can be too rich, sand can hold too much water and gravel provides no nutrients.

What else can you do?

After you have finished observing the plants, find a good place for the healthy ones in a garden so that they have a chance to flourish.

Wood-Louse House

45 minutes

You probably have a house that's dry, warm and provides light – but would that suit other animals?

The plan

We are going to find out what sort of conditions woodlice like to live in!

You will need:

- 5 cardboard boxes (approximately the same size and shape, such as tissue boxes)
- 4 cardboard tubes, 2 plastic bags
- 2 pieces of cardboard, plastic wrap
- paper towels, tape, marker
- at least 15 live wood lice (look under stones)
- scissors, water, notebook, pin

What to do:

1 Place a cardboard tube on the long side of a tissue box. Draw around the tube with a marker.

2 Cut out the circle with scissors. Repeat the process on three more boxes. On the last box you will need to mark and cut out a hole in each side.

3 Cut out the top of all five boxes, leaving a 4-inch (10 mm) border around the edge. Mark the boxes A, B, C, D and E.

4 Line the bases of all the boxes with plastic cut from a grocery bag, then put in two layers of paper towel. Dampen the paper in boxes A and B.

5 Stretch plastic wrap over boxes A and C. Use thick cardboard, cut to the right size, to cover boxes B and D. Use tape to secure the covers.

16

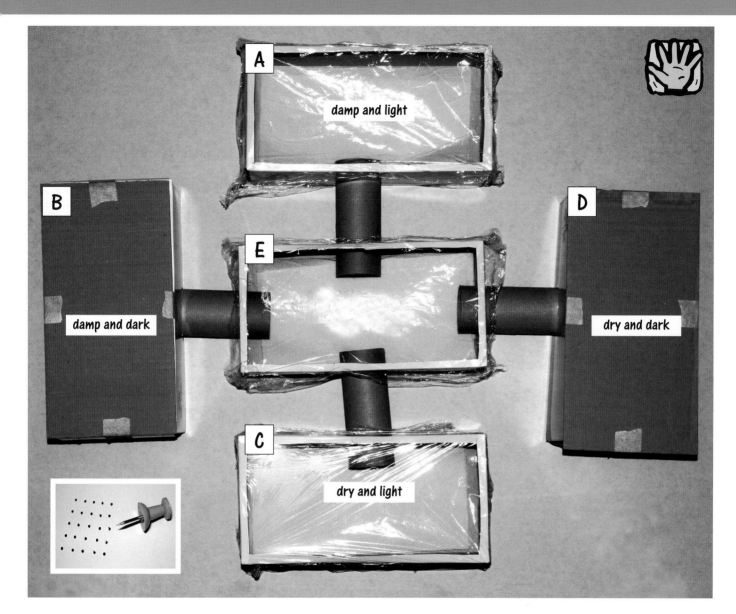

A
damp and light

B
damp and dark

E

D
dry and dark

C
dry and light

6 Push the tubes into each box and connect them as shown in the photograph above. Secure the tubes with tape. Make pin holes in the sides of all the boxes for air (see inset picture above).

7 Place the wood lice in box E, and cover the box with plastic wrap. Over four days, carefully check the numbers of wood lice in each outer box to see which one they prefer! Make notes of results.

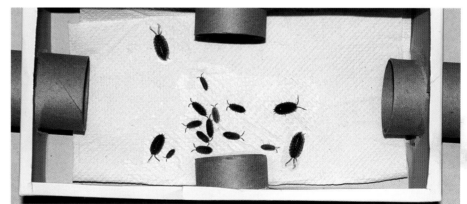

What's going on?

Like plants, animals are adapted to different living conditions – what is good for one could be *fatal* to another.

Very important!

Put the wood lice back where you found them once you have finished *observing* them!

A Wormery

60 minutes

We know that worms live under the ground. What do they do there? And why are they popular with gardeners?

You will need:

- 2 sheets of clear plastic about 12 inches (300 mm) square
- 3 pieces of wood 1 x 2 inches (25 x 50 mm):
  1 piece 12 inches (300 mm)
  2 pieces 11 inches (275 mm)
- strong waterproof tape
- rubber cement, scissors
- sand, soil, leaves, grass and earthworms

The plan

We are going to make a wormery that allows us to see what is going on under ground.

What to do:

1 *Assemble* the parts of the wormery as shown here.

2 Lay one sheet of plastic down, put the longest piece of wood at the base. Secure with rubber cement. Add the two sides.

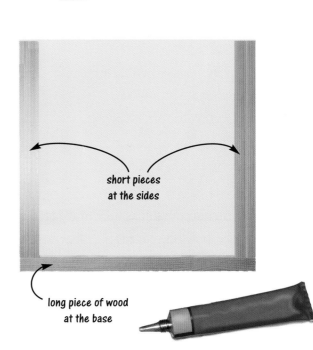

short pieces at the sides

long piece of wood at the base

Jargon Buster
Lumbricus terrestris is the scientific name for the earthworm.

3 Allow the glue to dry. Spread more glue on the surface of the wooden frame to secure the second piece of plastic. This completes the box. But you can also tape all around the frame for extra *stability*.

4 Add soil and sand in 1-inch (25 mm) layers. Dampen the sand with water. Put the worms on the top layer. Add some leaves and bits of grass for food. Keep the soil damp and do not overwater.

5 Observe the wormery over several days and weeks. Make notes about the results.

soil
sand
soil
sand
soil
sand
soil
sand

worms move the layers around

worms drag the leaves under ground

What's going on?

The worms mix up the soil as they move around and feed. They also break up lumps of soil and dry leaves, which become food for plants. Their burrows allow air into the soil, which also helps break down plant material. All these activities improve the soil, so most gardeners like worms in their garden.

What else can you do?

Put tiny pieces of grated vegetables on the top layer to check if your worms like a varied diet!

Very important!

When your experiment is finished, return your worms to the place you found them.

Microorganisms

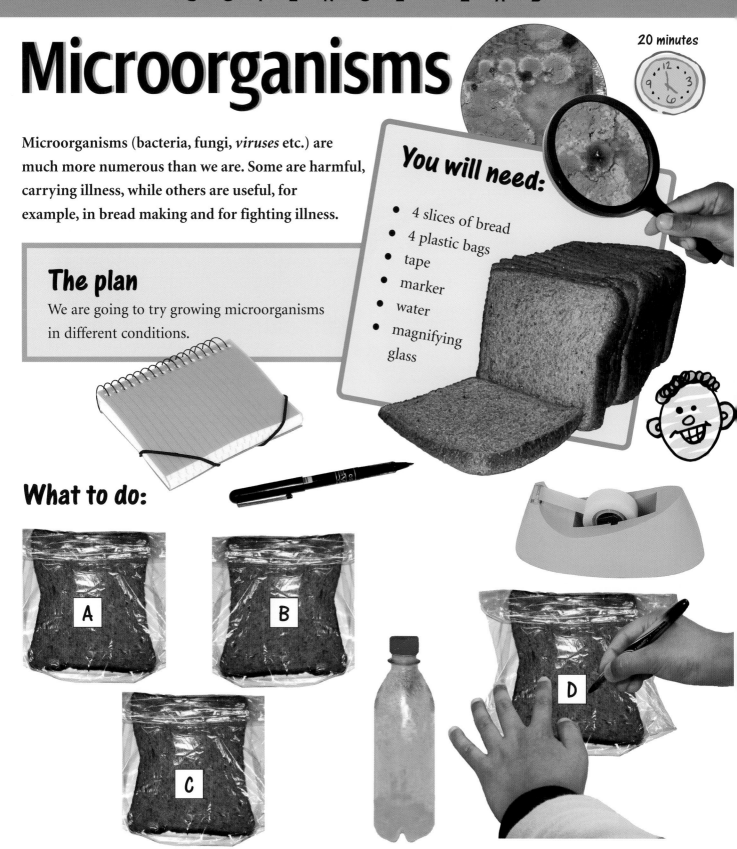

Microorganisms (bacteria, fungi, *viruses* etc.) are much more numerous than we are. Some are harmful, carrying illness, while others are useful, for example, in bread making and for fighting illness.

The plan

We are going to try growing microorganisms in different conditions.

You will need:

- 4 slices of bread
- 4 plastic bags
- tape
- marker
- water
- magnifying glass

What to do:

1 Put three slices of bread into three separate plastic bags marked A, B and C. Seal the ends with tape.

2 Dampen the fourth slice of bread with water and put it into the plastic bag marked D. Seal with more tape.

A
no light

B
no light
no warmth

3 Put bag A into a dark place, such as a cupboard.

4 Put bag B into a fridge.

C
warm and
light

D
warm, light
and damp

5 Put bag C and bag D into the same warm, light place. Examine all the bags daily but DO NOT OPEN THE BAGS.

6 Record amount and color of mold in a notebook. Check the mold through the plastic with magnifying glass.

What's going on?

Molds are a type of fungus. All fungi like warm, dark places. As we have been learning, living things are adapted for a wide range of conditions.

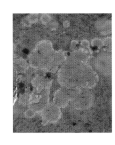

What else can you do?

See the next page for more experiments to find out where microorganisms will grow!

WARNING!

Do not breath in spores. Wash your hands often.

More Microorganisms

You will need:

- empty plastic water bottle
- tape
- 4 jars of water
- string
- hole punch
- scissors, teaspoon
- plasticine, 4 popsicle sticks
- food – jam, marmalade, ketchup, mustard or similar (DO NOT USE ANIMAL PRODUCTS)

The plan

We're going to find out what happens with different foods in water.

What to do:

1 Cut four strips of plastic from an empty water bottle. Make each 1 x 3 inches (25 x 75 mm).

2 Make a hole at the end of each strip with a hole punch. Tie a 4-inch (100 mm) string to each strip.

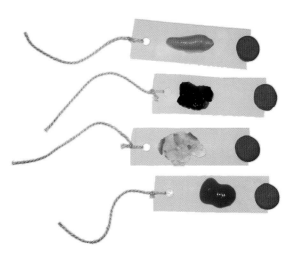

3 Add a lump of plasticine on each strip as a weight.

4 Spread half a teaspoon of one food on each strip.

jam   mustard   ketchup   marmalade

5 Fill the jars with water. Carefully lower each strip into the water. Tie the string to a popsicle stick.

6 Observe what happens to the food samples each day for a week. Keep notes in your notebook.

What's going on?

Some microorganisms are adapted to live in water. Check samples with a magnifying glass, through the jar. Note which food gets attacked first.

Warning!

Get rid of all samples and jars safely after use. Wash your hands frequently. Avoid contamination with other food.

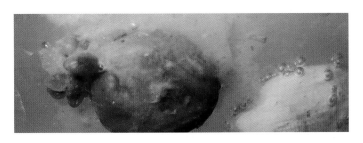

Jargon Buster
Contamination means spoiling something by adding another material to it.

Sight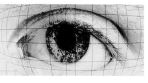

20 minutes

So far we have experimented with some of the living things in the world around us. But we are alive, too, and we can also experiment on ourselves!

You will need:

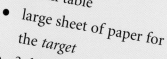

- small table
- large sheet of paper for the *target*
- 3 different-colored thick markers, a jar lid
- scissors and thin cardboard for the spinner
- pencil, glue stick
- string

The plan

We are going to learn a bit about how our eyes work and how using two eyes is often better than one!

Experiment 1

1 Draw your target on paper and put it flat on a table.

2

 **Cover one eye.**
To test your aim, hold a marker with the top removed at arm's length. Try to drop it on the center of the target.

 **Cover the other eye.**
Repeat the test and try to hit the target with the next marker.

 Use both eyes.
Repeat the test with the last pen.

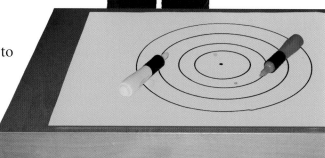

Experiment 2

1 Draw around a jar lid with a marker. Cut out two disks from your cardboard to make a spinner.

2 Draw a simple bird cage on one disk and a black bird on the other one. Stick the disks together, back to back, with one drawing upside down.

3 Make a hole on each side of the cardboard and tie a string to each hole. Holding the strings, flip the circle so that the strings twist over and over.

4 Pull the strings tight so that the disk spins back and forth quickly. As you watch, you will see the two drawings combine – now the bird is in the cage!

What's going on?

In experiment 1, are some marks off target? Each eye sees things from a slightly different angle. The brain compares the two different images and figures out how far away objects are. With only one eye, it cannot do this.

In experiment 2, an image of what we see remains on the retina of the eye for a fraction of a second after the object disappears. Because the movement of the disk is so rapid, the image is still there when it has spun around, so we see both sides of the disk at once.

Jargon Buster

Stereoscopic vision is possible thanks to the close side-by-side positioning of our eyes. Each sees the same area from a slightly different angle. The eye views have plenty in common, but each eye picks up visual information the other doesn't.

Hearing

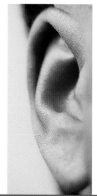

The sense of hearing has qualities that we often take for granted. Here's an experiment that shows how our ears help us find our way around.

You will need:

- a friend to be the subject
- 16 feet (5 m) of plastic hose
- 2 plastic funnels
- blindfold
- notebook, pen or pencil
- 4 more friends

Get friends to help you!

The plan

We're going to see how well we can tell the direction a noise is coming from without relying on our eyes.

What to do:

1 Cut the hose in half. Push a funnel into each hose.

2 Get a friend or classmate to stand in an open space. Put a blindfold around his eyes. He now becomes subject A for your hearing experiment! Position the other people around him without letting the subject know where they are.

3 In turn, each person claps their hands together once. After each clap the subject must point in the direction of the noise. Do they guess ✓ right or ✗ not?

Clap!

Clap!

Clap!

Clap!

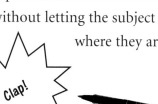

Subject A		Subject B	
1	✓	1	✗
2	✓	2	✓
3	✗	3	✓
4	✓	4	✗
5	✗	5	✗

4 Write down the results in your notebook to compare with the answers in the next part.

5 Keep the subject blindfolded. He becomes subject B. Ask the subject to hold the ends of both the hoses to his ears. Get two people to each hold a funnel and point it in different directions.

6 Repeat step 3, but this time the subject must turn to face the direction from which he thinks the noise is coming. Record the answers in your notebook.

7 Compare your results for steps 3 and 6. What difference do the hoses and funnels make to the answers?

What's going on?

Just as we have stereoscopic vision, we also have stereophonic hearing, which in a similar way helps us to identify the direction from which a sound is coming.

What else can you do?

Test how easy it is to find the direction of a sound with only one ear. Put a hand over the other ear. Then get a friend to help you find the direction of the sound with the hose and funnel!

Jargon Buster
Subject means the person selected to be the main part of the experiment.

Touch

Touch is another important sense we rely on to keep us safe. It lets us experience sensations like hot and cold, rough and smooth, wet and dry, soft and hard.

The plan

To see if your friends can identify hidden objects by feel and touch alone.

What to do:

1 Cut two holes big enough to get your fist through in the sides of the cardboard box. Decorate the box with colored shapes or markers.

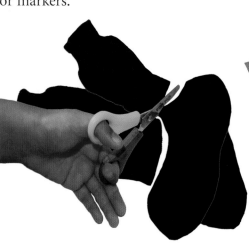

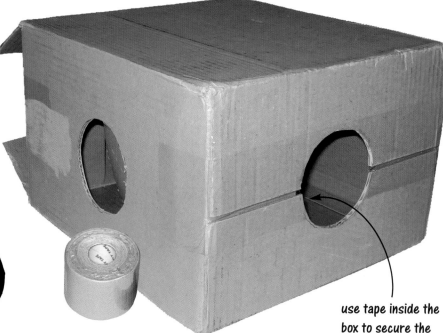

use tape inside the box to secure the sock sleeve

2 Cut the straight parts off two old black socks (ask for some before you destroy dad's best socks). Use strong tape to secure them to the inside of the box so they make "sleeves" coming out of the box. Put your hands through the socks to feel the objects in the box without seeing them.

Experiment 1

1 Things to try in the box: spoon, tennis ball, toys, fruit, pencil, thread spool, pine cone, sunglasses, slipper, brush, tin foil, keys, oven mitt, empty match box and so on.

2 Put several things in the box at the same time, without anyone else seeing. You can either have two people playing using one hand each or one person using both hands.

3 Ask how many items are in the box. To help them guess what each object is, ask questions: "Is it heavy?" "Is it light?" Discuss how the objects feel: smooth, rough, soft, hard and so on. Record results to see who gets the most right.

Experiment 2

Wearing a pair of rubber gloves, each person has another try using different objects. Again, everyone tries to guess what is in the box. Compare the results with experiment 1.

What's going on?

You can now judge what happens when you reduce the amount of tactile (touch) information getting to your brain. Just relying on what you can feel can be really tricky!

Taste and Smell

Seventy to seventy-five percent of what we think is taste actually comes from our sense of smell. Taste buds allow us to recognize only a few flavors. It's the odor molecules from food that give us most of our taste sensations!

You will need:

- 4 different flavors of potato chips
- blindfold
- notebook and pencil
- some friends

The plan

We're going to see how well people can tell which foods they're eating by only relying on the senses of taste or smell.

A	B	C	D
sour cream & onion	salt & vinegar	spicy	plain

What to do:

1 Blindfold one friend. Ask him to pinch his nose while he tastes each item.

2 Repeat the experiment with the other people. Keep notes to compare the results.

What's going on?

We can really only taste four things: bitter, salty, sweet and sour. Much of what we think we taste, we actually smell!

Jargon Buster

A **molecule** is the smallest particle into which something can be divided without chemical change.
Odor molecules produce particular smells.

A B C D

Glossary

animal products   (A-nuh-mul PRAH-dukts) Foods that come from animals, such as meat, eggs, butter, milk and cheese.

approximately   (uh-PROK-suh-mut-lee) Fairly exact.

assemble   (uh-SEM-bel) To arrange in an ordered way; put items together correctly.

bacteria   (bak-TIR-ee-uh) A large group of single cell organisms, some of which cause illnesses.

burrow   (BUR-oh) A hole or tunnel dug by a small animal making a home.

chlorophyll   (KLOR-uh-fil) The chemical that green plants use to help make their food.

compost   (KOM-pohst) Decayed organic material used as a fertilizer for growing plants.

develop   (dih-VEH-lup) To grow and become larger or more advanced.

evaporates   (ih-VA-puh-rayts) Turns from a liquid into a vapor.

fatal   (FAY-tul) Causing death to a plant or animal.

fungi   (FUN-jy) Plural of "fungus", spore-producing organisms that feed on organic matter.

funnel   (FUH-nul) Cone-shaped item used to assist with pouring liquids into narrow bottles.

gravity   (GRA-vih-tee) The force that pulls things toward the center of the Earth.

identical   (eye-DEN-tih-kul) Exactly alike, the same as.

magnifying   (MAG-nuh-fy-ing) Making something appear larger, in this case with the use of a lens.

nutrients   (NOO-tree-unts) Things that provide food needed for life and growth.

observing   (ub-ZERV-ing) Watching something very carefully.

preference   (PREH-fernts) A greater liking for one thing over another or others.

record   (rih-KORD) To make a note of and keep for the future.

scattering   (SKA-tur-ing) Throwing in various directions.

seedlings   (SEED-lingz) Seeds that have just sprouted leaves and roots, becoming small plants.

stability   (stuh-BIH-luh-tee) In this case, held together securely.

target   (TAHR-git) A round board with concentric rings to be aimed at.

thrive   (THRYV) To do well, to develop correctly.

transplant   (TRANZ-plant) To move to another place or to replant.

viruses   (VY-rus-ez) Submicroscopic particles that cause infection.

Index

compost

Web Sites

Due to the changing nature of Internet links, PowerKids
Press has developed an online list of Web sites related to
the subject of this book. This site is updated regularly.
Please use this link to access the list:
www.powerkidslinks.com/scilab/living/

FEB   2010